First World War
and Army of Occupation
War Diary
France, Belgium and Germany

14 DIVISION
43 Infantry Brigade,
Brigade Trench Mortar Battery
21 August 1915 - 30 July 1916

WO95/1910/6

The Naval & Military Press Ltd
www.nmarchive.com
Published in association with The National Archives

Published by

The Naval & Military Press Ltd

Unit 10 Ridgewood Industrial Park,

Uckfield, East Sussex,

TN22 5QE England

Tel: +44 (0) 1825 749494

www.naval-military-press.com

www.nmarchive.com

This diary has been reprinted in facsimile from the original. Any imperfections are inevitably reproduced and the quality may fall short of modern type and cartographic standards.

Contents

Document type	Place/Title	Date From	Date To
Heading	WO95/1910/6 14 Div-43 Inf Bde. Bde TM Batty-Aug 1915-Jul 1916		
Heading	43 Trench Mortar Bty 1915 Aug To 1916 July		
War Diary	In the Field	21/08/1915	09/10/1915
War Diary	Field.	18/10/1915	24/10/1915
War Diary		24/10/1915	21/11/1915
War Diary	In the Field	21/11/1915	28/11/1915
War Diary		18/12/1915	19/12/1915
War Diary	I 33 C 0.8	20/12/1915	31/12/1915
War Diary	43 Trench Motar Bty Jan 1916 Vol VIII		
War Diary	Field.	01/01/1916	29/01/1916
War Diary	Field.	15/02/1916	29/02/1916
War Diary	Field.	01/03/1916	05/03/1916
War Diary	Field	01/03/1916	31/03/1916
War Diary	In the Field.	01/04/1916	30/04/1916
War Diary	Field.	05/04/1916	30/04/1916
War Diary	Field.	05/04/1916	29/04/1916
War Diary	Field	05/04/1916	30/04/1916
War Diary	Field	29/04/1916	30/04/1916
War Diary	In the Field	01/04/1916	17/04/1916
War Diary	In the Field	01/04/1916	30/04/1916
War Diary	In the Field	13/04/1916	27/05/1916
War Diary	Field.	28/05/1916	31/05/1916
War Diary	In the Field	01/05/1916	10/05/1916
War Diary	Field.	11/05/1916	31/05/1916
War Diary	In the Field.	01/05/1916	12/05/1916
War Diary	In the Field	01/05/1916	27/05/1916
War Diary	In the Field	13/05/1916	30/05/1916
War Diary	In the Field	01/05/1916	10/05/1916
War Diary	Field.	11/05/1916	31/05/1916
War Diary	In the Field	01/05/1916	11/05/1916
War Diary	In the Field	01/06/1916	30/06/1916
War Diary	Field.	01/06/1916	23/06/1916
War Diary	Field	01/06/1916	23/06/1916
War Diary	Field	11/06/1916	30/06/1916
War Diary	In the Field.	01/06/1916	27/06/1916
War Diary	In the Field	01/06/1916	30/06/1916
War Diary	In the Field	25/06/1916	30/06/1916
War Diary	Field.	01/06/1916	23/06/1916
War Diary	Field.	01/07/1916	22/07/1916
War Diary	In the Field.	23/07/1916	30/07/1916
War Diary	Field	01/07/1916	22/07/1916
War Diary	Field	01/07/1916	30/07/1916
War Diary	In the Field	23/07/1916	30/07/1916

WO95/1910 - 6

14 Div - 43 Inf Bde.

Bde T M Batty

Aug 1915 - Jul 1916

~~2 ARMY TROOPS~~

~~14 DIV 43 Bde~~

43

TRENCH MORTAR

BTY

1915 AUG TO 1916 JLY

~~1604~~

Instructions regarding War Diaries and Intelligence Summaries are contained in F. S. Regs., Part II. and the Staff Manual respectively. Title Pages will be prepared in manuscript.

WAR DIARY
or
INTELLIGENCE SUMMARY
(Erase heading not required.)

Army Form. C. 2118

43rd J.H.B.

5,000 — Imp. des A. C. — 24/7/15

Place	Date	Hour	Summary of Events and Information	Remarks and references to Appendices
In the field	Aug 21st		Battery formed and taken from School to join 3rd Division. Billetted and attached for administrative purposes with 40. Brigade A.C.	
	" 22nd		In billets: gun drill and telephone class.	
	" 23rd		Lt. Forsyth 2/Lt. Haskins and Sergt. Haviland reconnoitred for positions at HOOGE and found positions N. of MENIN ROAD. Battery still in billets. —	
	" 24th		Visited C.R.A and 7th Inf. Brigade to which we were attached. Ordered into action and at nightfall went to ECOLE at YPRES with A. and B. detachments.	
	" 25.		At 3.30 a.m had two guns in action on HOOGE front: visited Brigade H.Q. and Wilts. Ordered not to fire unless enemy opened. Quiet day, did not fire. —	
	" 26		Thoroughly reconnoitred the area and found alternative positions and gave orders to have the necessary work done. At 6p.m registered enemy's trenches at N.W. of BELLEWARDE LAKE; had one air burst so ordered all fuzes to be set at 28 unless special orders given. Enemy did not retaliate.	
	" 27		Between 3a.m and 5a.m fired five rounds at trenches previously registered: and 3 rounds at trenches N. of Chateau and near edge of LAKE. One round fell 24 yards short: Possibly a faulty gas check but cannot explain otherwise as range they appeared correct. — One round failed to completely detonate but it was not blind. — Having regard to small amount of ammunition arranged to have one detachment only and one officer always in trenches one detachment in reserve about ½ mile back and 2 detachments in rest. This works out as 3 days per detachment in trenches, 3 days in reserve, and six in rest. Two men sleep by each gun and the officer near by.	Copy C1
	" 28		Fired nine rounds at enemy's works near Bellewarde Lake. Enemy working hard. Fired at night. One blind.	JK 2/9/15

Instructions regarding War Diaries and Intelligence Summaries are contained in F. S. Regs., Part II. and the Staff Manual respectively. Title Pages will be prepared in manuscript.

WAR DIARY
or
INTELLIGENCE SUMMARY
(Erase heading not required.)

Army Form. C. 2118

Week ending 12 noon Sunday Sept 5th

Sheet I

5,000 — Imp. des A. C. — 24735

Place	Date	Hour	Summary of Events and Information	Remarks and references to Appendices
	Aug 29th		"B" Sect relieved "A" Sect. A quiet day ~~A quiet day~~ Found a new position to fire behind Chateau & put a gun in; did not fire at request of R.I.R.	
	Aug 30th		Fired six rounds at dawn into enemy trenches, 3 behind Chateau and 3 in wood near Eclusette. At 6 pm fired 4 rounds on trenches along the lake. Had to cease fire as enemy shelled ridge very heavily for 3/4 hour. At night dug a new emplacement south of road so as to fire on Hooge Wall.	
	Aug 31st		Between 12 + 1 pm fired 5 rounds to register the Eclusette, one blind. At 6 pm fired 4 rounds to register Hooge wall. A quiet day. "C" + "D" relieved "A" + "B" Sections who went to rest. "C" Section came to trenches, "D" in reserve.	
	Sept 1st		At 3.30 am fired 3 rounds on Hooge Wall & trenches behind. Our artillery opened fire at 4 am. + enemy replied vigorously. During the bombardment fired 4 rounds on wood near Eclusette. A quiet day. At night dug a new position behind present line for future occasion; the work will take some days to complete	
	Sept 2nd		Our artillery opened fire at 3.55 am. Enemy bombarded us heavily. Fired 10 rounds on enemy trenches near lake & Eclusette. Private McLardy slightly wounded, Gunner West shaken by bursting shell. 2/Lt Hankins relieved Lt. Forsyth who was proceeding on leave to England on Sept 3rd	

Instructions regarding War Diaries and Intelligence Summaries are contained in F. S. Regs., Part II. and the Staff Manual respectively. Title Pages will be prepared in manuscript.

WAR DIARY
or
INTELLIGENCE SUMMARY
(Erase heading not required.)

Army Form. C. 2118

5,000 — Imp. des A. C. — 24715

Place	Date	Hour	Summary of Events and Information	Remarks and references to Appendices
	~~Aug~~ Sept 2nd (cont)		From 4 to 6 pm enemy heavily bombarded our trenches. Both guns and all ammunition in the trenches were buried. Gunner Peddie + Private Deans were killed, Sergt Haviland admitted to hospital for nervous breakdown.	
			Detachments withdrawn to échelle during remainder of Lt Forsyth's leave.	
	Sept 3rd		During the morning artillery fire was heavy from both sides.	
			50 rounds of ammunition received from 40th Brigade Am. Col.	
	Sept 3rd to Sept 5th noon		Nothing of importance was done; an unsuitable gun position was made but no firing took place. Subsequently G.O.C. 9th Inf. Bde ordered the gun to be moved further forward.	
			W Forsyth Lt RFA	
				JF 20/9/15

Army Form. C. 2118

Instructions regarding War Diaries and Intelligence Summaries are contained in F. S. Regs., Part II. and the Staff Manual respectively. Title Pages will be prepared in manuscript.

WAR DIARY
or
INTELLIGENCE SUMMARY
(Erase heading not required.)

43rd T. M. Bty.

Place	Date	Hour	Summary of Events and Information	Remarks and references to Appendices
	Sept 12th		At 2.30 am fired 2 rounds at Eclusette also Q 61 (Reference Special Hooge Map). At 7.30 ~~fired~~ fired at Eclusette, one round and hit it and made Germans run. Firing from lower Hooge ridge at 12. so retaliated with 8 rounds. Between 6 + 7 pm. registered enemies second line trench North of Menin Rd. and supposed trench Mortar position. Fired four rounds no reply by enemy. During night a Magazine was dug about 400x from Gun positions under bank of Menin Road. C+D. relieved A+B in trenches	
	Sept 13th		worked to strengthen position and began to prepare another emplacement as enemy Bombardment was expect about 10.30 am stood to. It was a very mild affair fired 1 round	
	Sept 14th		Gunner Garvey J. was appointed acting Bombardier. Fired 8 rounds at Eclusette: 1 Blind two short, 5 very effective, also 4 at Q 61. 3 effective 1 Blind. fired between 4.30 and 6.30	
	Sept 15th		Battery went into rest having no Ammunition. Left a guard on Gun positions	
	Sept 16th		Visited the School in the morning, and Gen: Hoskins in afternoon. All men had Baths.	
	Sept 17th – 18		Battery in rest.	[initials] 20/9

[signature] 2/Lt R.F.A.

Army Form. C. 2118

Instructions regarding War Diaries and Intelligence Summaries are contained in F. S. Regs., Part II. and the Staff Manual respectively. Title Pages will be prepared in manuscript.

WAR DIARY
or
INTELLIGENCE SUMMARY
(Erase heading not required.)

43rd Trench Mortar Bty

Place	Date	Hour	Summary of Events and Information	Remarks and references to Appendices
	Sept 17th to 21st	–	Battery at Rest. Saw C.R.A. and G.O.C. 7th Infantry Brigade.	
	Sept 22nd	–	Ammunition taken to Hooge (128 rds) and dumped. – B. Gun emplacement damaged by Shell fire. Cpl Wilkinson proceeded on Leave.	
	Sept 23rd	–	Visited Hooge with No. 1. and at night, had damaged emplacement repaired, and C. Position completed. Battery went up to Ecole.	
	Sept 24th		Orders for operation received, and all necessary arrangements made; Went into action with 3 Detachments, 1 in reserve. Visited G.O.C. 7th Inf. Bde. and arranged to be attached to 2nd S. Lancs. –	
	Sept 25th		At appointed time 3·50 am. opened fire with all 3 Guns. During Bombardment Cpl Hother No. 1. of A Gun was killed by shell exploding in the Gun, both Man & Gun being blown to pieces. (Cause unknown) Remainder of Det: suffering from severe shock. Lt S.S. Forsyth was Killed about 6 am. shot through the head. B. Gun put out of action. (Rifle Mec: struck by piece of shell) remaining Gun being buried. Cpl McCallum took charge & retired in the evening after reporting to O.C. South Lancs. Lt Hankins arrived at Ecole and took Command at 11 pm and then proceeded to the trenches. 68 Rds received from 40th Bde A.C.	
	Sept 26th		About 2 am D. Gun was got into action, fired 8 Rds on Chateau at 6-30 pm. The Gun buried, was recovered and put in action at night close to B Gun position. ~~heavy~~ heavy Bombardment between 10-30 - 11-30 pm. At this period only 1 N.C.O and 11 Men available for Duty, several reporting sick.	

G.A. Hankins 2Lt R.G.A.
Officer Comdg 43rd T M Bty

3/10/15

Instructions regarding War Diaries and Intelligence Summaries are contained in F. S. Regs., Part II. and the Staff Manual respectively. Title Pages will be prepared in manuscript.

WAR DIARY
or
INTELLIGENCE SUMMARY
(Erase heading not required.)

Army Form. C. 2118

43rd Trench Mortar Battery
3rd Division.
Week ending Oct. 2nd 1915

5,000 — Imp. des A. C. — 24.7.15

Place	Date	Hour	Summary of Events and Information	Remarks and references to Appendices
Sept. 26th	Sept 26th		Ammunition recovered and sorted out during the day. 8 rounds fired at chateau at 5.30 pm. After dark B gun emplacement repaired and gun brought into action. Heavy bombardment at 10-30 to 11.30 pm.	
	Sept 27th		Quiet day, did not fire on orders from infantry. Engaged in repairing trenches. Gnr Woodhead on leave	
	Sept 28th		~~Did no~~ 24th 40th & 43rd T M Batteries combined in two groups 43rd Battery forms part of Left Group. 2/Lt Hankins in charge of Left Group which consists of 2 - 4" & 1 - 2" Trench Mortars. 5 rounds of ammunition dug out of old C emplacement. Corpl Wilkinson returned off leave and came up to trenches	
	Sept 29th		Gun not required in action sent back to billets. Did not fire on orders from infantry. New gun & new firing mechanism received from school. Damaged parts sent back.	
	Sept 30th		Quiet day, did not fire. Heavy artillery & bomb attacks on our right	
	Oct. 1st		Quiet day, did not fire on orders from infantry	
	Oct 2nd		As yesterday. 2/Lt Hankins went back to billets at night, Sergt Simnett left in charge with approval of C. R. A.	
			JK 2/10/15	
			G A Hankins 2/Lt. R.G.A. O.C. 43 T.M. Btty.	

Instructions regarding War Diaries and Intelligence Summaries are contained in F. S. Regs., Part II. and the Staff Manual respectively. Title Pages will be prepared in manuscript.

WAR DIARY
or
INTELLIGENCE SUMMARY
(Erase heading not required.)

Army Form. C. 2118.

43rd Trench Mortar Battery

Place	Date	Hour	Summary of Events and Information	Remarks and references to Appendices
In the field	1915 Oct 3rd		Quiet Day. Enemies Mortars fired. Sergt Simmett did not reply as Infantry asked for Artillery who silenced enemies Mortars.	
	Oct 4th		Quiet Day, did not fire. engaged in making position strong at night.	
	Oct 5th		As yesterday. Lt Hankins relieved Sgt Simmett in trenches who returned to billets	
	Oct 6th		as yesterday. did not fire on orders from Infantry	
	Oct 7th		as yesterday. did not fire. Lt McGuinness Smith arrived at trenches and took charge Lt Hankins receiving orders to see the C.R.A.	
	Oct 8th		Lt Hankins left trenches at 7 am. Quiet day did not fire	
	Oct 9th		Lt Hankins left for England receiving Orders from C.R.A. Men were relieved at trenches by men at Billets did not fire	

[initials] 12/10/15

C. McGuinness Smith Lt N Staff Regt
O.C. 43 T.M. Bty

October.

Instructions regarding War Diaries and Intelligence Summaries are contained in F. S. Regs., Part II. and the Staff Manual respectively. Title Pages will be prepared in manuscript.

WAR DIARY
or
INTELLIGENCE SUMMARY
(Erase heading not required.)

43rd Trench Mortar Battery

Army Form. C. 2118.

5,000 — Imp. des A. C. — 24/7/15

Place	Date	Hour	Summary of Events and Information	Remarks and references to Appendices
Field.	18th	-	Nothing to report.	
	19	-	Quiet day. No firing.	
	20	-	Quiet day.	
	21	-	Improving gun emplacements and dug-outs for the winter. A number of German hand bombs dug-out in the vicinity of a gun emplacement.	
	22	-	No firing.	
	23	-	Two new gun emplacements commenced.	
	24	-	2Lt. Dinwoodie relieved 2Lt. McGuinness Smith in the trenches.	

Sgd. McGuinness Smith 2Lt.
N. Clapp
Cmdg 43rd T.M. Battery.

Instructions regarding War Diaries and Intelligence Summaries are contained in F. S. Regs., Part II. and the Staff Manual respectively. Title Pages will be prepared in manuscript.

WAR DIARY
or
INTELLIGENCE SUMMARY
(Erase heading not required.)

Army Form. C. 2118.

43rd Batt & 1/2 37th Batty. Lt E. McGuinness Smith 2nd Lt. Cmdg 43rd G M B

Place	Date	Hour	Summary of Events and Information	Remarks and references to Appendices
Sunday	1915 24th Oct		Lt McG Smith was relieved by Lt Dinwoodie at 8 pm. Very quiet day did not fire	
Monday	25th Oct		Engaged in making ammunition recesses, Built up part of communication Trench The enemy very quiet in front they appeared to be improving their trenches which seemed to be in a bad condition did not fire	
Tuesday	26th Oct		Very quiet day, The Brigadier 30th Inf. Bde. sent for me to obtain information re. Trench Mortars, did not fire.	
Wednesday	27th Oct		Quiet day although snipers were at work and hit one or two Infantry men improved our works around the Mens dugouts.	
Thursday	28th Oct		Very Wet day, so could not do much work, improved the trenches as much as possible Enemy very quiet; did not fire, was relieved by Lt McG Smith at 7-30pm	[illegible] 3/1
Friday	29th		Enemy artillery very active during the day. Located one battery in the vicinity of J. 7C.44. and reported to H. Qrs. R.F.A. (80th Bde) Enemy hard at work along Hooge front. Trench Mortar activity very much suppressed in this quarter. Pte. A. Smith (R. Scots Fus.) wounded through the leg by rifle fire & sent to hospital.	
Saturday	30th	–	From 2 pm to 3 pm. enemy shelled in the neighbourhood of our trench mortar. No damage was done. No trench mortar firing	
Sunday	31st	–	A quiet day. A & C sections relieved B & D. No firing done.	

Instructions regarding War Diaries and Intelligence Summaries are contained in F. S. Regs., Part II. and the Staff Manual respectively. Title Pages will be prepared in manuscript.

WAR DIARY
or
INTELLIGENCE SUMMARY
(Erase heading not required.)

43rd Trench Mortar Bty.

Army Form. C. 2118

Place	Date	Hour	Summary of Events and Information	Remarks and references to Appendices
1st Nov.	1915	–	New emplacement commenced for B gun. Registered three rounds at 5 pm. on enemy works I 12 c. 91. (Special Hooge Map) All three were duds.	
2nd Nov.	1915	–	2 Lt Dinwoodie in trenches No firing done.	
3rd Nov.	1915	–	A Quiet day.	
4th Nov.	1915	–	Did no firing.	
5th Nov.	1915	–	2 Lt McGuinness Smith relieved 2 Lt. Dinwoodie.	
6th Nov.	1915	–	Lively artillery bombardment on both sides from 5 am to 7 am. At 6 am. Fired six rounds on I 12 c. 91. Two were duds, the rest very effective. Emplacement for B gun continued.	
7th Nov.	1915	–	B gun emplacement completed and gun brought into action. Intended registering B & C guns on Chateau positions at dusk but Infantry (Dorsets) did not want us to fire as trenches were in a bad state.	JK. 7/11/15

McGuinness Smith 2 Lt.
Cmdg. 43rd T. M. Bty.

Army Form. C. 2118

Instructions regarding War Diaries and Intelligence Summaries are contained in F. S. Regs., Part II. and the Staff Manual respectively. Title Pages will be prepared in manuscript.

WAR DIARY
or
INTELLIGENCE SUMMARY
(Erase heading not required.)

43rd T.M. Bty

5,000 — Imp. des A. C. — 24.7.15

Place	Date	Hour	Summary of Events and Information	Remarks and references to Appendices
8th Nov.	1915	–	At 3.30 pm. fired 6 rounds from 4" gun and 5 rounds from 2" gun on Chateau positions. 2. 4" were duds, and 4. 2" were duds, otherwise firing was good. At 4.15 pm. fired 4. 4" on Belvrette, of which one was a dud.	
9th Nov.	1915	–	At 6 am. fired 6. 4" and 3. 2" on enemy positions I.20d. 41-82. 1. 2" was a dud, the others effective. 2/Lt Rosnoodie relieved 2/Lt. McGuinness Smith same night.	
10th Nov.			At 3.31 pm the enemy fired over at intervals 10 aerial torpedoes. We retaliated by firing 12 rounds from the 4 in gun & 5 rounds from the 2 in gun. We had 2 duds & one air burst with the 4 in ammunition & 1 air burst from the 2 in gun.	R 21/11
11th Nov.			Made two new gun emplacements and repaired the trenches	
12th Nov.			Repaired the trenches which were in a bad condition	
13th Nov.			Continued to repair the trenches and dugouts. The enemy shelled us vigorously from 12 noon till 5 pm. Lt was relieved by 2/Lt Gen G Smith	
14th Nov.		–	Quiet day. No firing done. New dug-out commenced.	

2/Lt. McGuinness Smith 2/Lt
Comdg. 43. T.M. Bty

Army Form. C. 2118

Instructions regarding War Diaries and Intelligence Summaries are contained in F. S. Regs., Part II. and the Staff Manual respectively. Title Pages will be prepared in manuscript.

WAR DIARY
or
INTELLIGENCE SUMMARY

(Erase heading not required.)

43. J. H. Batty.

Place	Date	Hour	Summary of Events and Information	Remarks and references to Appendices
Monday.	15th Nov.		No firing done. Work carried out in trenches & new dug-out:	
Tuesday	16th Nov.		Quiet day. Battery withdrawn at night & replaced by 27th Battery. 43rd Battery at rest.	
	17th to 21st		Battery at rest.	

G. E. McGuinness Smith 2Lt.

Instructions regarding War Diaries and Intelligence Summaries are contained in F. S. Regs., Part II. and the Staff Manual respectively. Title Pages will be prepared in manuscript.

WAR DIARY
or
INTELLIGENCE SUMMARY
(Erase heading not required.)

Army Form. C. 2118

43rd Trench Mortar Battery 30/11

5,000 — Imp des A. C. — 24 7 15

Place	Date	Hour	Summary of Events and Information	Remarks and references to Appendices
In the field	from 21st 11/15 to 28 11/15		Battery at rest in Billets at R11 a 4.6. Sheet 27. Physical Drill & Semaphore Daily.	
			G. E. McGuinness Smith. 2/Lt Officer Comdg 43 T.M. Bty	

Instructions regarding War Diaries and Intelligence Summaries are contained in F. S. Regs., Part II. and the Staff Manual respectively. Title Pages will be prepared in manuscript.

WAR DIARY
or
INTELLIGENCE SUMMARY
(Erase heading not required.)

48th T.M. Battery

Army Form. C. 2118

Place	Date	Hour	Summary of Events and Information	Remarks and references to Appendices
	Dec		On Saturday 18th inst I proceeded to "Spoilbank" with a	
			party of 6 men for the purpose of building a dugout. At Dickebusch	
	18		Dump I loaded the waggon with 7 iron girders 200 ft of timber &	
			20 sheets of corrugated iron. which was dumped outside	
	19		the mess dugout. On the 19th inst we excavated the hole	
			in the bank size 18ft x 7ft. The 20th soil was wet and in	
I33	20		consequence the walls of the dugout ~~fell~~ in in places	
			making the work very difficult. The ration waggon that	
	21		night brought up some more timber. The next day we	
			continued the work of revetting the sides with expanded metal	
	22		and heavy timber. We next put the roof on and	
			strengthened the sides of the dugout & doorway with timber	
	23		wire netting & sandbags. On the 24th inst two men came	
			up bringing with them felt & canvas nails etc and timber for the	
			flooring. This was carried to the Dump by an infantry fatigue.	
	24		I then took my party back to the billets leaving the dugout	
			in charge of the two men. During the whole time we were	

Instructions regarding War Diaries and Intelligence Summaries are contained in F. S. Regs., Part II. and the Staff Manual respectively. Title Pages will be prepared in manuscript.

WAR DIARY
or
~~INTELLIGENCE~~ SUMMARY
(Erase heading not required.)

Army Form. C. 2118

43rd T M Batty 1⁄3/1

5,000 — Imp. des A. C. — 24 7/15

Place	Date	Hour	Summary of Events and Information	Remarks and references to Appendices
	25.12.15		The B attery remained in Billets for ~~the~~ Christmas Day.	
	26.12.15		The half battery proceeded to the trenches again taking with them 2 guns and 24 rounds of ammunition the waggons also called at the Dickebusch Dump and obtained a supply of timber for finishing the Dugouts.	
	27.12.12		On the 27th inst the Officers Dugout was finished and lined with Canvas. and the men started enlarging their dugout and flooring it	
	28.12.15		One half of the men under Br Mellbourne. proceeded to make the emplacements while the other half improved the paths outside the dugouts and laid a telephone wire to Btn Hqrs.	
	29.12.15		One emplacement was finished and another one started on the 29th inst. while the dugout roofs ~~were~~ were covered with turf & foliage to conceal it from enemy aircraft.	
	30.12.15			

Instructions regarding War Diaries and Intelligence Summaries are contained in F. S. Regs., Part II. and the Staff Manual respectively. Title Pages will be prepared in manuscript.

WAR DIARY
or
INTELLIGENCE SUMMARY
(Erase heading not required.)

Army Form. C. 2118

43rd T M Batty

5,000 — Imp. des A. C. — 24 7 15

Place	Date	Hour	Summary of Events and Information	Remarks and references to Appendices
38.	30.12.15		13 Gun Emplacement was finished and the paths outside the dugouts were drained and improved.	
	31.12.15		A sandbag traverse was build up outside the Officers dugout doorway and ~~the~~ both dugouts were cleaned up ready for the relief ~~At~~ 6 pm I was relieved by Lieut McGuinness Smith. —	~~43rd TMB~~

H Dinwoodie. Lieut
43rd T M Batty

17?

43 Trench Mortar Bty

Jan 1916

Vol VII

43rd Trench Mortar Bty

Instructions regarding War Diaries and Intelligence Summaries are contained in F. S. Regs., Part II. and the Staff Manual respectively. Title Pages will be prepared in manuscript.

WAR DIARY
or
INTELLIGENCE SUMMARY
(Erase heading not required.)

43rd T.M. Battery.

Army Form C. 2118

[initials] 11/1/16

Place	Date	Hour	Summary of Events and Information	Remarks and references to Appendices
Field.	1916. Jan	1.	At 6.30 am enfiladed enemy's trench running along South bank of Canal with 8 rounds from A gun. Two were dudds. Some material damage was observed along the trench. At 3.30 pm registered 6 rounds on supposed redoubt at O.3.b.7.1. from B gun. No dudds. At night A & C sub-sections relieved B & D sub-sections.	
"	Jan	2.	At 7.30 am. fired 10 rounds from B gun at O.3.b.7.1. One was a dudd; others had effect on enemy's wire. At 11 am. registered 6 rounds from A gun on sniper's post and erection at O.3.b.5.1.	
"	Jan	3	At 7 am. fired 10 rounds from A gun on yesterday's registration at O.3.b.5.1. One dudd. Good results were observed. Enemy retaliated vigorously.	
"	Jan	4	In retaliation to enemy's trench mortars, fired 9 rounds from C gun at 5:30 pm. on mound at I.34 d.2.6. There was one dudd. Enemy's trench mortar was located about I.34 d.2.4, and it was firing on the Bluff.	

Contd.

Instructions regarding War Diaries and Intelligence Summaries are contained in F. S. Regs., Part II. and the Staff Manual respectively. Title Pages will be prepared in manuscript.

WAR DIARY
or
INTELLIGENCE SUMMARY
(Erase heading not required.)

43rd T.M. Battery

Army Form. C. 2118

Place	Date	Hour	Summary of Events and Information	Remarks and references to Appendices
Field	Jan.	5.	No firing was done. New emplacements were being prepared.	
"	Jan.	6	Did no firing. Work was being carried out in connection with a big shoot to-morrow morning. B & D sub-sections relieved A & C.	
"	Jan.	7	At 9.20 am C & D guns were in action on the salient at I 34 d. C kept up a continuous fire of 30 rounds. D was firing at a slower rate and expended 40 rounds before 11 am. At 10.35 am A gun fired 10 rounds at foot-bridge at O. 4 a. 8.8. This gun had a jam early in the shoot and was put out of action. Firing on the whole was observed to be excellent; and the salient was well searched by our guns.	

8/1/16

G.M.E. McGuinness Smith.
O.C. 43rd T.M. Battery.

Instructions regarding War Diaries and Intelligence Summaries are contained in F. S. Regs., Part II. and the Staff Manual respectively. Title Pages will be prepared in manuscript.

WAR DIARY
or
INTELLIGENCE SUMMARY
(Erase heading not required.)

43rd T. M. Battery.

Army Form. C. 2118

Place	Date	Hour	Summary of Events and Information	Remarks and references to Appendices
Field.	Jan.	8.	No firing was done. Instructions received to go slow as no more 4" Ammunition in Corps.	
"	"	9.	Did not fire. Work carried out on emplacements.	
"	"	10	At 3.30 pm. fired 15 rounds each from C & D guns in conjunction with 40th Battery on dug-outs in Area I34d.6.7. Attention was also given to I34d. point 26, reported as Cupola.	
"	"	11	There was no Trench Mortar activity on either side.	
"	"	12	At 2 pm. fired 12 rounds from C gun on large dug-out and supposed sap-head about I34d.0.6½. Infantry reported shooting as very accurate. Expanded metal and waterproof sheeting were seen to have been thrown right out of the trench.	
"	"	13	There was no firing.	
"	"	14.	2 Lt. Dinwoodie relieved Lt. McGuinness Smith at night.	
"	"	15	No firing done.	

McGuinness Smith Lt.
O.C. 43rd T.M.B.

Instructions regarding War Diaries and Intelligence Summaries are contained in F. S. Regs., Part II. and the Staff Manual respectively. Title Pages will be prepared in manuscript.

WAR DIARY
or
~~INTELLIGENCE SUMMARY~~
(Erase heading not required.)

Army Form. C. 2118

43rd T. M. Battery.

Place	Date	Hour	Summary of Events and Information	Remarks and references to Appendices
	16th		At 6pm I relieved Lt McGuinness Smith in the trenches	
	17th		Started building a new dugout for the men by the side of their old one. In the afternoon I fired 11 rounds at I 34 d 05	
	18		The work was continued on the dugout all day and in the evening the men were relieved by the other half battery.	
	19		At 10 30 AM we fired 6 rounds at I 34 d 05.06 in conjunction with 8 in Howitzer Batty. 18 pndr Batty & Belgian Batty. In the afternoon work was resumed on the dugout.	
	20th		Work was again carried out on mens new dugout during the	
	21		day and in the evening 36 rounds of ammunition were carried up from the Dump to the dugout.	
	22		We continued working on the dugout in the morning & in the afternoon we fired 7 rounds on the enemy trenches at I 34 d 05.	
	23		In the morning we carried material for the dugout from the Infantry dump and in the afternoon we fired 9 rounds on the enemy lines – dugouts at I 34 d 04.05.	
	24.		During the morning work was resumed on the mens dugout. At 1 pm I was relieved by Lt Smith.	

Army Form. C. 2118

Instructions regarding War Diaries and Intelligence Summaries are contained in F. S. Regs., Part II. and the Staff Manual respectively. Title Pages will be prepared in manuscript.

WAR DIARY
or
INTELLIGENCE SUMMARY
(Erase heading not required.)

43rd T. M. Battery. [illegible]

5,090 — Imp. des A. C. — 24/7/15

Place	Date	Hour	Summary of Events and Information	Remarks and references to Appendices
Field.	24th	Jan.	Lt. McGuinness Smith relieved 2 Lt. Dinwoodie in trenches. At 4 pm fired 6 rounds from C gun on Salient at I.34 d. 0.7. Enemy retaliated vigorously and stopped our firing.	
	25th	"	No firing. New emplacement for B gun commenced at I.34 C. 2.5½.	
	26th	"	No firing. Emplacements improved.	
	27th	"	Do. " "	
	28th	"	New emplacement for C gun commenced at I. 34. C. 3.7.	
	29th	"	Registered B gun with 3 rounds 4" on enemy first line and C.T opposite the BLUFF about O.4a. 9.9½. Two 3.7" Mortars taken into action, owing to shortage of 4" Ammunition.	

30/1/16.

McGuinness Smith, Lt.
O.C. 43rd T.M. Bty.

Instructions regarding War Diaries and Intelligence Summaries are contained in F. S. Regs., Part II. and the Staff Manual respectively. Title Pages will be prepared in manuscript.

WAR DIARY
or
INTELLIGENCE SUMMARY
(Erase heading not required.)

43rd T.M. Bty.

Army Form. C. 2118

5,000 — Imp. des A. C. — 24 7/15

Place	Date	Hour	Summary of Events and Information	Remarks and references to Appendices
Field	Feb. 15/16.		Called up from rest area and attached to 17th DIV.	
	Feb. 20 to Feb. 29.		Four 4" guns and two ~~S~~Stokes' guns were being prepared for action for offensive on the BLUFF.	

G.W. Guinness Smith, Lt.
O.C. 43rd T.M. Bty.

Instructions regarding War Diaries and Intelligence Summaries are contained in F. S. Regs., Part II. and the Staff Manual respectively. Title Pages will be prepared in manuscript.

WAR DIARY 43rd T.M. Bty
or
~~INTELLIGENCE SUMMARY~~
(Erase heading not required.)

Army Form. C. 2118

Place	Date	Hour	Summary of Events and Information	Remarks and references to Appendices
Field.	March 1st		Registered all guns on objectives preparatory to evenings bombardment.	
			At 5 pm. bombarded for 1 hour. Ammunition expended. 4" — 50, Stokes - 288.	
	March 2nd & 3rd		Trench mortared all through the early hours of the morning. Assault took place at ~~4 am.~~ 4.30 am. Ammunition expended. 4" - 42, Stokes - 76. Trench mortars in this offensive proved very successful. Battery sustained 4 casualties.	
			8018. L/Cpl. A. Page. 1st R. Scots. Fus. wounded. 7729. L/Cpl. W. Mackay. do. missing. } 43rd T.M. Bty.	
			9494. Cpl. Hardwick. 2nd W. Yorks. killed. 17680. Pte. Williams. 3rd W. Yorks. wounded. } Stokes detachment attd. 43rd T.M. Bty.	
	March 4th & 5th		No firing was done. Enemy heavily bombarded our positions.	

Capt. [illegible] Smith, Lt.
O.C. 43rd T.M. Bty.

Instructions regarding War Diaries and Intelligence Summaries are contained in F. S. Regs., Part II. and the Staff Manual respectively. Title Pages will be prepared in manuscript.

WAR DIARY
or
INTELLIGENCE SUMMARY
(Erase heading not required.)

43/1 Trench Mortar Battery

Army Form C. 2118.

Place	Date	Hour	Summary of Events and Information	Remarks and references to Appendices
Field	1·3·16		This Battery was formed at the IIIrd Army Trench Mortar School on the first of March & were trained on the 3·75" Trench mortar until the 8th of March.	JBJC
	8·3·16		The Battery equipped with four of 3·75" guns left the school on this date & proceeded by rail from Candas to Saulty & thence to Dainville by road	JBJC
	12·3·16		The Battery went into Action in the 43rd Infantry Brigade area & emplacements & dugout were made for the guns.	JBJC
	16·3·16		One gun fired three rounds for registration on a German sap leading from the Franchees Jocast. The time between the 16th & 22nd inst was spent in improving the positions & building bomb stores & dugouts for the men.	JBJC
	22·3·16		Eight rounds were fired on the enemies barrier ~~across~~ across the Ficheuse Road. Owing to the fact that a mine listening post was being dug near this position the position had to be evacuated.	JBJC
	27·3·16		Six rounds were fired in offensive fire on the enemies trenches at Franchees Malvaux.	JBJC

Army Form C. 2118.

Instructions regarding War Diaries and Intelligence Summaries are contained in F. S. Regs., Part II. and the Staff Manual respectively. Title Pages will be prepared in manuscript.

WAR DIARY
or
INTELLIGENCE SUMMARY
(Erase heading not required.)

Place	Date	Hour	Summary of Events and Information	Remarks and references to Appendices
Fula	29.3.16		Twelve rounds were fired on the "Tracks" Jocaste	JWJC.
	30.3.16		On the 30th 15 rounds were fired into the German Sap At 11am the enemy were seen working in his sap. Six rounds were fired & the working ceased.	JWJC.
	31.3.16		Eight rounds were fired today on the German Sap off the "Tracks" Jocaste with good result	JWJC.

J. Jenner Clarke Lt.
O.C. 43/1 Trench Mortar Battery

'1'

Instructions regarding War Diaries and Intelligence Summaries are contained in F. S. Regs., Part II. and the Staff Manual respectively. Title Pages will be prepared in manuscript.

WAR DIARY
or
~~INTELLIGENCE SUMMARY~~

(Erase heading not required.)

Army Form C. 2118.

43/1 Trench Mortar Batt
14 Div.

Place	Date	Hour	Summary of Events and Information	Remarks and references to Appendices
In the Field	1.4.16		On this date eight rounds were fired onto the enemies' front line at a point called Tranchée Jocaste.	JMC
	2.4.16		Ten rounds were fired onto the German saps running from the Tranchée Jocaste	JMC
	3.4.16		Ten rounds were again fired onto the German front line & saps	JMC
	4.4.16		Ten rounds were fired onto the enemy front line	JMC
	5.4.16		Nine rounds were fired again onto the same point	JMC
	6.4.16		On this date two rounds were fired onto the Tranchée Jocaste.	JMC
	7.4.16		Ten rounds were fired this day onto the German front line & saps.	JMC
	8.4.16		Twelve rounds were fired onto the German front line six of which were fired at a working party in a sap opening. The Germans the work at once ceased	JMC
	9.4.16		No. one gun position had to be moved owing to an M.G. emplacement having been built in front of this position. Another position was found & work was commenced on it. No rounds were fired on the day	JMC
	10.4.16		The day was spent in registering new gun & improving the position & building bomb store. Five rounds were fired	JMC
	11.4.16		The position was finished on this day & ten rounds were fired	JMC
	12.4.16		No work was done owing to bad weather.	JMC

2449 Wt. W14957/M90 750,000 1/16 J.B.C. & A. Forms/C.2118/12.

'2'

Instructions regarding War Diaries and Intelligence Summaries are contained in F. S. Regs., Part II. and the Staff Manual respectively. Title Pages will be prepared in manuscript.

WAR DIARY
or
INTELLIGENCE SUMMARY
(Erase heading not required.)

Army Form C. 2118.

43/1 Trench Mortar Batt
14 Div.

Place	Date	Hour	Summary of Events and Information	Remarks and references to Appendices
[illegible]	12.4.16		The day was spent in working on No 3 position. No rounds were fired.	JWC
	14.4.16		No 3 position was completed but owing to bad weather no rounds were fired	JWC
	15.4.16		Thirteen rounds fired & dugout [illegible] on No 3 gun [illegible]	JWC
	16.4.16		Bomb slit on No 3 gun finished & ten rounds fired	JWC
	17.4.16		Twenty rounds were fired onto German saps & front line	JWC
	18.4.16 / 19.4.16		Owing to bad weather no firing was done.	JWC
	20.4.16		Ten rounds were fired causing heavy retaliation	JWC
	21.4.16		Twenty rounds were fired in a shoot with Z/14 Medium TM Batt.	JWC
	22.4.16 / 23.4.16 / 24.4.16		Owing to high winds on the day no rounds were fired.	JWC
	25.4.16		The day was spent in registering new position	JWC
	26.4.16		At 11.45 pm a round was fired falling near an MG the gun stopped firing at once & did not fire during the rest of the night.	JWC
	27.4.16		During the afternoon [illegible] of the guns fired with the 2" TM & fired at intervals throughout the night in the hope of catching any party which might be repairing the damage done by the afternoon bombardment.	JWC
	29.4.16		We fired in a shoot with the 2" & firing at intervals throughout the night.	JWC
	30.4.16		Ten rounds were fired at the German [illegible] & [illegible] at the Tranchée [illegible].	JWC

[illegible] OC 43/1 TMB.

2449 Wt. W14957/M90 750,000 1/16 J.B.C. & A. Forms/C.2118/12.

Instructions regarding War Diaries and Intelligence Summaries are contained in F. S. Regs., Part II. and the Staff Manual respectively. Title Pages will be prepared in manuscript.

WAR DIARY
or
~~INTELLIGENCE SUMMARY~~
(Erase heading not required.)

Army Form C. 2118.

43/2 Trench Mortar Battery
14th Division

Place	Date	Hour	Summary of Events and Information	Remarks and references to Appendices
Field.	1916 Apl 5th		– This Battery was formed and proceeded to Trench Mortar School III Army, for a course of instruction in the use of 3" Stokes T.M's.	JH.
"	– 12th		– The Course was completed on the 12th Apl, & the battery left T.M. School equipped with 4 - 3" Stokes T.M, proceeding to DAINVILLE preparatory to going into action.	JH.
"	13th to 18th		– On the 13th positions were selected & battery proceeded into action in area of 43rd Brigade, 14th Div. VI Corps.	JH.
			– Apl 13 to 18th were spent in making emplacements, and bringing guns into action.	JH.
			– Owing to the issue of Red Cartridges being stopped, the efficiency of these guns were greatly handicapped, as 300x is the extreme range of the Green Cartridges.	JH.
"	26th		– Two Gun position registered.	JH.
			– During the next few days, firing was very difficult, owing to weather.	JH.
	28th		– Another Gun position registered.	JH.
	29th		– Firing three guns on registered positions, & concentrated on enemy's barrier on railway. ~~[illegible]~~ JH	JH

2449 Wt. W14957/M90 750,000 1/16 J.B.C. & A. Forms/C.2118/12.

Army Form C. 2118.

Instructions regarding War Diaries and Intelligence Summaries are contained in F. S. Regs., Part II. and the Staff Manual respectively. Title Pages will be prepared in manuscript.

WAR DIARY
or
~~INTELLIGENCE SUMMARY~~
(Erase heading not required.)

43/2 Trench Mortar Battery
14th Division

Place	Date	Hour	Summary of Events and Information	Remarks and references to Appendices
Field	29th	10pm	Night firing was carried out from three guns on enemy saps & a portion of front line. - A working party was dispersed & a machine gun silenced. (32 rounds being fired) Enemy retaliated with T.M.s but 8 rounds silenced him..	JH
	30th		10 rounds fired in retaliation to enemy's Trench Mortars.	JH

Field
Apl 30th 1916.

J Hetherington Lt
OC. 43/2 Trench Mortar Battery

2449 Wt. W14957/M90 750,000 1/16 J.B.C. & A. Forms/C.2118/12.

Army Form C. 2118.

Instructions regarding War Diaries and Intelligence Summaries are contained in F. S. Regs., Part II. and the Staff Manual respectively. Title Pages will be prepared in manuscript.

WAR DIARY
or
~~INTELLIGENCE SUMMARY~~
(Erase heading not required.)

43/2 Trench Mortar Battery
14th Division

Place	Date	Hour	Summary of Events and Information	Remarks and references to Appendices
Field.	1916 Apl 5th		– This Battery was formed and proceeded to Trench Mortar School III Army, for a course of instruction in the use of 3" Stokes T.M's.	JH.
"	-12th		– The Course was completed on the 12th Apl, & the battery left T.M. School equipped with 4 - 3" Stokes T.M, proceeding to DAINVILLE preparatory to going into action.	JH.
"	13th to 18th		– On the 13th positions were selected & battery proceeded into action in area of 43rd Brigade, 14th Div. VI Corps.	JH.
			– Apl 13 to 18th were spent in making emplacements, and bringing guns into action.	JH.
			– Owing to the issue of Red Cartridges being stopped, the efficiency of these guns were greatly handicapped, as 300x is the extreme range of the Green Cartridges.	JH.
"	26th		– Two gun position registered.	JH.
			– During the next few days, firing was very difficult, owing to weather.	JH.
"	28th		– Another gun position registered.	JH.
"	29th		– Firing three guns on registered positions, & concentrated on enemy's barrier on railway. ~~[illegible]~~ JH	JH

2449 Wt. W14957/M90 750,000 1/16 J.B.C. & A. Forms/C.2118/12.

Army Form C. 2118.

Instructions regarding War Diaries and Intelligence Summaries are contained in F. S. Regs., Part II. and the Staff Manual respectively. Title Pages will be prepared in manuscript.

WAR DIARY
or
INTELLIGENCE SUMMARY
(Erase heading not required.)

43/2 Trench Mortar Battery
14th Division

Place	Date	Hour	Summary of Events and Information	Remarks and references to Appendices
Field.	1916 Apl 5th		– This Battery was formed and proceeded to Trench Mortar School III Army, for a course of instruction in the use of 3" Stokes T.M's.	JH.
	– 12th		– The Course was completed on the 12th Apl. & the battery left T.M. School equipped with 4 · 3" Stokes T.M. proceeding to DAINVILLE preparatory to going into action.	JH.
	13th to 18th		– On the 13th positions were selected & battery proceeded into action in area of 43rd Brigade, 14th Div. VI Corps.	JH.
			– Apl 13 to 18th were spent in making emplacements, and bringing guns into action.	JH.
			– Owing to the issue of Red Cartridges being stopped, the efficiency of these guns were greatly handicapped, as 300x is the extreme range of the Green Cartridges.	JH.
	26th		– Two gun position registered.	JH.
			– During the next few days, firing was very difficult, owing to weather.	JH.
	28th		– Another gun position registered.	JH.
	29th		– Firing three guns on registered positions & concentrated on enemy's barrier on railway. ~~[illegible]~~ JH	JH.

2449 Wt. W14957/M90 750,000 1/16 J.B.C. & A. Forms/C.2118/12.

Army Form C. 2118.

Instructions regarding War Diaries and Intelligence Summaries are contained in F. S. Regs., Part II. and the Staff Manual respectively. Title Pages will be prepared in manuscript.

WAR DIARY
or
~~INTELLIGENCE SUMMARY~~
(Erase heading not required.)

43/2 Trench Mortar Battery
14th Division

Place	Date	Hour	Summary of Events and Information	Remarks and references to Appendices
Field	29th	10pm	Night firing was carried out from three guns on enemys saps & a portion of front line. - A working party was dispersed & a machine gun silenced. (32 rounds being fired) Enemy retaliated with T.M.s but 8 rounds silenced him..	JH
	30th		10 rounds fired in retaliation to enemys Trench Mortars.	JH

Field
Apl 30th 1916.

J Hetherington Lt
OC 43/2 Trench Mortar Battery

2449 Wt. W14957/M90 750,000 1/16 J.B.C. & A. Forms/C.2118/12.

Army Form C. 2118.

Instructions regarding War Diaries and Intelligence Summaries are contained in F. S. Regs., Part II. and the Staff Manual respectively. Title Pages will be prepared in manuscript.

WAR DIARY
or
~~INTELLIGENCE SUMMARY~~
(Erase heading not required.)

43/2 Trench Mortar Battery
14th Division

Place	Date	Hour	Summary of Events and Information	Remarks and references to Appendices
Field	29th	10pm	Night firing was carried out from three guns on enemy saps & a portion of front line. – A working party was dispersed, & a machine gun silenced. (32 rounds being fired) Enemy retaliated with T.M.s but 8 rounds silenced him..	JH
	30th		10 rounds fired in retaliation to enemy Trench Mortars.	JH

Field
Apl 30th 1916.

J Hetherington Lt
OC 43/2 Trench Mortar Battery

Instructions regarding War Diaries and Intelligence Summaries are contained in F. S. Regs., Part II. and the Staff Manual respectively. Title Pages will be prepared in manuscript.

WAR DIARY
or
INTELLIGENCE SUMMARY
(Erase heading not required.)

Army Form C. 2118.

43/1 Trench Mortar Batt.
14 Div.

Dupl

Place	Date	Hour	Summary of Events and Information	Remarks and references to Appendices
In the Field	1.4.16		On this date eight rounds were fired onto the enemy front line at a point called Tranchée Jocaste.	JHC.
	2.4.16		Ten rounds were fired onto the German saps running from the Tranchée Jocaste	JHC
	3.4.16		Ten rounds were again fired onto the German front line & saps	JHC.
	4.4.16		Ten rounds were fired onto the enemy front line	JHC.
	5.4.16		Nine rounds were fired again onto the same point.	JHC.
	6.4.16		On this date ten rounds were fired onto the Tranchée Jocaste.	JHC.
	7.4.16		Ten rounds were fired this day onto the German front line & saps.	JHC.
	8.4.16		Twelve rounds were fired onto the German front line six of which were fired at a working party in a sap opposite the Corinth the work at once ceased	JHC.
	9.4.16		No one gun position had to be moved owing to an M.G. emplacement having been built in front of this position. Another position was found & work was commenced on it. No rounds were fired on this day.	JHC.
	10.4.16		The day was spent in registering new gun & improving the position & building bomb stores. Five rounds were fired	JHC.
	11.4.16		The position was finished on this day & ten rounds were fired	JHC.
	12.4.16		No work was done owing to bad weather.	JHC

Army Form C. 2118.

WAR DIARY
or
INTELLIGENCE SUMMARY
(Erase heading not required.)

43/1 Trench Mortar Batt.
14 Div.

Instructions regarding War Diaries and Intelligence Summaries are contained in F. S. Regs., Part II. and the Staff Manual respectively. Title Pages will be prepared in manuscript.

Place	Date	Hour	Summary of Events and Information	Remarks and references to Appendices
In the Field	1.4.16		On this date eight rounds were fired onto the enemies front line at a point called Tranchée Jocaste.	[initials]
	2.4.16		Ten rounds were fired onto the German saps running from the Tranchée Jocaste	[initials]
	3.4.16		Ten rounds were again fired onto the German front line & saps.	[initials]
	4.4.16		Ten rounds were fired onto the enemy front line	[initials]
	5.4.16		Nine rounds were fired again onto the same point.	[initials]
	6.4.16		On this date two rounds were fired onto the Tranchée Jocaste.	[initials]
	7.4.16		Ten rounds were fired this day onto the German front line & saps.	[initials]
	8.4.16		Twelve rounds were fired onto the German front line six of which were fired at a working party in a sap adjoining the Tranchée the work at once ceased.	[initials]
	9.4.16		No. one gun position had to be moved owing to an M.G. emplacement having been built in front of this position. Another position was found & work was commenced on it. No rounds were fired on this day.	[initials]
	10.4.16		The day was spent in registering new gun & improving the position & building bomb store. Five rounds were fired	[initials]
	11.4.16		The position was finished on this day & ten rounds were fired	[initials]
	12.4.16		No work was done owing to bad weather.	[initials]

'2'

Instructions regarding War Diaries and Intelligence Summaries are contained in F. S. Regs., Part II. and the Staff Manual respectively. Title Pages will be prepared in manuscript.

WAR DIARY
or
~~INTELLIGENCE SUMMARY~~ 43/1 Trench Mortar Batt 14 Div.

(Erase heading not required.)

Army Form C. 2118.

Place	Date	Hour	Summary of Events and Information	Remarks and references to Appendices
In the Field	13.4.16		The day was spent in working on No 3 position. No rounds were fired	JWJC
	14.4.16		No 3 position was completed but owing to bad weather no rounds were fired	JWJC
	15.4.16		Thirteen rounds fired & dugout ~~[illegible]~~ on No 3 gun finished	JWJC
	16.4.16		Bomb store on No 3 gun finished & ten rounds fired	JWJC.
	17.4.16		Twenty rounds were fired onto German saps & front line	JWJC.
	18.4.16 19.4.16	}	Owing to bad weather no firing was done.	JWJC.
	20.4.16		Ten rounds were fired causing heavy retaliation	JWJC.
	21.4.16		Twenty rounds were fired in a shoot with Z/14 Medium TM Batt.	JWJC.
	22.4.16 23.4.16 24.4.16	}	Owing to high winds on this day no rounds were fired.	JWJC.
	25.4.16		The day was spent in registering new position	JWJC
	26.4.16		At 11.45 pm a round was fired falling near an MG the gun stopped firing at once & did not fire during the rest of the night.	JWJC.
	27.4.16		During the afternoon the one of the guns fired with the 2" TM & fired at intervals throughout the night in the hope of catching any party which might be repairing the damage done by the afternoon bombardment.	JWJC.
	29.4.16		We fired in a shoot with the 2" & firing at intervals throughout the night.	JWJC
	30.4.16		Ten rounds were fired at the German sap & front line at the [illegible].	JWJC.

2449 Wt. W14957/M90 750,000 1/16 J.B.C. & A. Forms/C.2118/12.

Army Form C. 2118.

WAR DIARY
or
INTELLIGENCE SUMMARY
(Erase heading not required.)

X3/1 Trench Mortar Batt
14 Div.

Instructions regarding War Diaries and Intelligence Summaries are contained in F. S. Regs., Part II. and the Staff Manual respectively. Title Pages will be prepared in manuscript.

Place	Date	Hour	Summary of Events and Information	Remarks and references to Appendices
[illegible]	13.4.16		The day was spent in working in No 3 position. No rounds were fired	JWC
	14.4.16		No 3 position was completed but owing to bad weather no rounds were fired	JWC
	15.4.16		Thirteen rounds fired & dugout finished on No 7 gun position	JWC
	16.4.16		Bomb store on No 3 gun finished & ten rounds fired	JWC.
	17.4.16		Twenty rounds were fired into German saps & front line	JWC.
	18.4.16		Owing to bad weather no firing was done.	JWC.
	19.4.16			
	20.4.16		Ten rounds were fired causing heavy retaliation	JWC.
	21.4.16		Twenty rounds were fired in a shoot with Z/14 Medium T.M. Batt.	JWC.
	22.4.16		Owing to high winds in the day no rounds were fired	JWC.
	23.4.16			
	24.4.16		The day was spent in registering new position	JWC.
	25.4.16			
	26.4.16		At 11.45 pm a round was fired falling near an MG the gun stopped firing at once & did not fire during the rest of the night.	JWC.
	27.4.16		During the afternoon three of the guns fired with the 2" T.M. & fired at intervals throughout the night in the hope of hitting any party which might be repairing the damage done by the afternoon bombardment	JWC.
	29.4.16		We fired in a shoot with the 2" & firing at intervals throughout the night.	JWC
	30.4.16		Ten rounds were fired at the German cap & front line at the Trench [illegible]	JWC.

J. W. [illegible] Clarke 2/Lt
[illegible]

2449 Wt. W14957/M90 750,000 1/16 J.B.C. & A. Forms/C.2118/12.

43/1 Trench Mortar Battery

Instructions regarding War Diaries and Intelligence Summaries are contained in F. S. Regs., Part II. and the Staff Manual respectively. Title Pages will be prepared in manuscript.

XIV

WAR DIARY
or
~~INTELLIGENCE SUMMARY~~
(Erase heading not required.)

43/1 TM B~~G~~

Vol 3

Army Form C. 2118.

Place	Date	Hour	Summary of Events and Information	Remarks and references to Appendices
In the Field	1.5.16		This battery joined in a shoot carried out by the medium Batteries in the evening of the 1st. A good result seems to have been produced. The enemy retaliated heavily	JWC
	3.5.16		The right gun fired four rounds into a point in the German line called the Tranchée Jocaste. The centre gun fired 7 rounds in retaliation to the enemies Trench Mortars. The left gun fired 17 rounds onto the enemies towers across the Fincky Road & onto the trenches in the vicinity of the towers.	JWC
	4.5.16		The right gun fired four rounds onto the Tranchée Jocaste. The centre gun fired 13 rounds onto the Saps & Tranchée Jocaste in retaliation to the enemies Trench Mortars. The left gun fired 9 rounds onto the enemies towers in retaliation.	JWC
	5.5.16		A reserve position was sighted & commenced on this date. 35 rounds were fired.	JWC
	6.5.16		No firing or work carried out owing to bad weather	JWC
	7.5.16		No rounds fired owing to bad weather	JWC
	8.5.16		Six rounds were fired at the Tranchée Jocaste	JWC
	9.5.16		Gun positions & bomb store completed	JWC
	12.5.16		Thirteen rounds were fired onto the enemies Saps leading from the Tranchée Jocaste & onto the Tranchée Jocaste	JWC

H 3/1 Trench Mortar Battery

Instructions regarding War Diaries and Intelligence Summaries are contained in F. S. Regs., Part II. and the Staff Manual respectively. Title Pages will be prepared in manuscript.

WAR DIARY
or
~~INTELLIGENCE SUMMARY~~
(Erase heading not required.)

Army Form C. 2118.

II

Place	Date	Hour	Summary of Events and Information	Remarks and references to Appendices
In the Field	13.5.16		No firing was done owing to bad weather.	JBC
	14.5.16		Six rounds were fired on the Tranchée Jocaste & 14 on the barrier across the Feuchy Road.	
	15.5.16		Ten rounds were fired in retaliation onto the Tranchée Jocaste & four onto the Barrier.	JBC
	16.5.16		Fifteen rounds were fired at the Feuchy Road barrier. Ten rounds were fired at the Tranchée Jocaste in retaliation to enemy Trench Mortars.	JBC
	17.5.16		No firing was carried out owing to bad weather.	JBC
	18.5.16		Nine rounds were fired in retaliation on the Tranchée Jocaste.	JBC
	19.5.16		No firing was carried out owing to bad weather.	JBC
	20.5.16		Seven rounds were fired at the Tranchée Jocaste today.	JBC
	21.5.16		Seven rounds were fired at the Feuchy Road barrier.	JBC
	22.5.16		Four rounds were fired at the Barrier.	JBC
	23.5.16		Six rounds were fired at the Feuchy Road barrier & trench in the vicinity of the barrier. These rounds called forth heavy retaliation from the German large trench mortar.	JBC
	24.5.16		Four rounds were fired at the Tranchée Jocaste.	JBC
	27.5.16		New position started for the four guns.	JBC

2449 Wt. W14957/M90 750,000 1/16 J.B.C. & A. Forms/C.2118/12.

III

Instructions regarding War Diaries and Intelligence Summaries are contained in F. S. Regs., Part II. and the Staff Manual respectively. Title Pages will be prepared in manuscript.

WAR DIARY
or
~~INTELLIGENCE SUMMARY~~

(Erase heading not required.)

Army Form C. 2118.

Place	Date	Hour	Summary of Events and Information	Remarks and references to Appendices
Field	28.5.16		New position finished	[illegible]
	29.5.16		A reserve position commenced.	[illegible]
	30.5.16		New position Registered	[illegible]
	31.5.16		New firing was carried out from new position. The results seem good. Small pieces of timber were observed to fly from the enemies trench	[illegible]

J.K. Jenner Clarke Lieut
OC 43/1 TMB.

2449 Wt. W14957/M90 750,000 1/16 J.B.C. & A. Forms/C.2118/12.

XIV

Instructions regarding War Diaries and Intelligence Summaries are contained in F. S. Regs., Part II. and the Staff Manual respectively. Title Pages will be prepared in manuscript.

WAR DIARY
or
~~INTELLIGENCE SUMMARY~~
(Erase heading not required.)

Army Form C. 2118.

43/2 Trench Mortar Battery

Vol 2

Place	Date	Hour	Summary of Events and Information	Remarks and references to Appendices
In the Field	1916 May 1.		During the day a new position was made & registered ready for a night shoot, in conjunction with 3.7 + 2" Batteries.	
			This Shoot took place about 10pm & was very successful.	JH
			The enemy retaliated with 77mm Shells, & heavy Shrapnel, but little material damage was done.	
	2nd & 3rd		Retaliation to Enemy's Trench Mortar.	JH
	4th		30 rounds fired in retaliation	
		2/30pm	A Combined Shoot took place (Stokes, 3.7 + 2" Medium) on the enemy front line, where new work had been in progress. The result was Satisfactory	JH.
	5th		New position built & registered on enemy's Sap. (M.14 d. 7½.4½ Sheet 51B. S.W.1)	JH
			43 rounds fired in retaliation.	
	6th		22 rounds fired in retaliation	JH
	7th 8th		No firing took place owing to weather	
	9th	10pm	Fired 6 rounds at enemy working party & dispersed them.	
	10th		Usual retaliation fire.	

Instructions regarding War Diaries and Intelligence Summaries are contained in F. S. Regs., Part II. and the Staff Manual respectively. Title Pages will be prepared in manuscript.

Army Form C. 2118.

WAR DIARY
or
~~INTELLIGENCE~~ SUMMARY
(Erase heading not required.)

43/2 Trench Mortar Battery

Place	Date	Hour	Summary of Events and Information	Remarks and references to Appendices
Field	11th	3pm.	1 Stokes Gun, T.1-3.7", fired on enemy Sap ~~M.d~~ (M14d. 7¼ · 4½). In the evening this was repeated, when enemy retaliated vigourously with heavy Shrapnel. It is supposed that a machine gun was put out of action, as no firing took place afterwards	JH
	12th to 21st		Usual retaliation fire.	
	22nd	5am,	Enemy fired for the first time, 1 large, + 1 medium MINENWERFER, apparently for the purpose of registering.	JH
			An enemy mine was discovered, under our front line. At request of General Cooper Cmdg 14th Div, 3 guns of this Battery were placed in defensive positions, in case the mine is exploded.	
	23rd to 31st		Retaliation fire.	
			Enemy large mortars active	

J Hetherington Lieut
OC 43/2 Trench Mortar Bty

Field
June 1st 1916

2449 Wt. W14957/M90 750,000 1/16 J.B.C. & A. Forms/C.2118/12.

43/1 Trench Mortar Battery

Instructions regarding War Diaries and Intelligence Summaries are contained in F. S. Regs., Part II. and the Staff Manual respectively. Title Pages will be prepared in manuscript.

WAR DIARY
or
~~INTELLIGENCE SUMMARY~~
(Erase heading not required.)

Army Form C. 2118.

Place	Date	Hour	Summary of Events and Information	Remarks and references to Appendices
In the Field	1.5.16		This battery joined in a shoot carried out by the Medium Batteries in the evening of the 1st. A good result seems to have been produced. The enemy retaliated heavily.	[illegible]
	3.5.16		The right gun fired four rounds into a point in the German line called the [illegible] Jocaste. The centre gun fired 7 rounds in retaliation to the enemy's Trench Mortars. The left gun fired 17 rounds onto the enemy's [illegible] across the Road & onto the trenches in the rear of [illegible].	[illegible]
	4.5.16		The right gun fired four rounds onto the Tranchée Jocaste. The centre gun fired 13 rounds onto the Saps & Tranchée Jocaste in retaliation to the enemy's Trench Mortars. The left gun fired 9 rounds onto the enemy['s] [illegible] in retaliation.	[illegible]
	5.5.16		A reserve position was sighted & commenced on this date. 36 rounds were fired.	[illegible]
	6.5.16		No firing or work carried out owing to bad weather	[illegible]
	7.5.16		No rounds fired owing to bad weather	[illegible]
	8.5.16		Forty rounds were fired at the Tranchée Jocaste.	[illegible]
	9.5.16		Gun position & bomb store completed	[illegible]
	12.5.16		Thirteen rounds were fired onto the enemy Saps leading from the Tranchée Jocaste & onto the Tranchée Jocaste.	[illegible]

2449 Wt. W14957/M90 750,000 1/16 J.B.C. & A. Forms/C.2118/12.

Instructions regarding War Diaries and Intelligence Summaries are contained in F. S. Regs., Part II. and the Staff Manual respectively. Title Pages will be prepared in manuscript.

WAR DIARY
or
INTELLIGENCE SUMMARY
(Erase heading not required.)

Army Form C. 2118.

Place	Date	Hour	Summary of Events and Information	Remarks and references to Appendices
[illegible]	[illegible]		[illegible]	[illegible]

H 3/1 Trench Mortar Battery

Army Form C. 2118.

WAR DIARY
or
~~INTELLIGENCE SUMMARY~~

(Erase heading not required.)

II

Instructions regarding War Diaries and Intelligence Summaries are contained in F. S. Regs., Part II. and the Staff Manual respectively. Title Pages will be prepared in manuscript.

Place	Date	Hour	Summary of Events and Information	Remarks and references to Appendices
In the Field	13.5.16		No firing was done owing to bad weather	[illegible]
	14.5.16		Six rounds were fired on the Tranchée [illegible] & 14 on the barrier across the Feuchy Road.	[illegible]
	15.5.16		Ten rounds were fired in retaliation onto the Tranchée [illegible] & four onto the Barrier	[illegible]
	16.5.16		Fifteen rounds were fired at the Feuchy Road barrier. Ten rounds were fired at the Tranchée [illegible] in retaliation to enemy Trench Mortars.	[illegible]
	17.5.16		No firing was carried out owing to bad weather.	[illegible]
	18.5.16		Nine rounds were fired in retaliation on the Tranchée [illegible]	[illegible]
	19.5.16		No firing was carried out owing to bad weather	[illegible]
	20.5.16		Seven rounds were fired at the Tranchée [illegible]	[illegible]
	21.5.16		Seven rounds were fired at the Feuchy Road barrier.	[illegible]
	22.5.16		Four rounds were fired at the Barrier	[illegible]
	23.5.16		Six rounds were fired at the Feuchy Road barrier & trench in the vicinity of the barrier. These rounds called forth heavy retaliation from the German large trench mortar	[illegible]
	24.5.16		Four rounds were fired at the Tranchée [illegible]	[illegible]
	27.5.16		New position started for the fourth gun.	[illegible]

2449 Wt. W14957/M90 750,000 1/16 J.B.C. & A. Forms/C.2118/12.

Army Form C. 2118.

Instructions regarding War Diaries and Intelligence Summaries are contained in F. S. Regs., Part II. and the Staff Manual respectively. Title Pages will be prepared in manuscript.

WAR DIARY
or
INTELLIGENCE SUMMARY
(Erase heading not required.)

Place	Date	Hour	Summary of Events and Information	Remarks and references to Appendices
In the Field	13.5.16		No firing was done owing to bad weather	
	14.5.16		Six rounds were fired on the Tranchée [illegible] and [illegible] at the barrier across the Faucky Road	[illegible]
	15.5.16		Ten rounds were fired in retaliation on the Tranchée [illegible] & four on the Barrier	[illegible]
	16.5.16		Fifteen rounds were fired at the Faucky Road barrier. Ten rounds were fired at the Tranchée [illegible] in retaliation to enemy trench mortars	[illegible]
	17.5.16		No firing was carried out owing to bad weather	[illegible]
	[illegible]		Nine rounds were fired in retaliation on the Tranchée [illegible]	[illegible]
	19.5.16		No firing was carried out owing to bad weather	[illegible]
	21.5.16		Seven rounds were fired at the Tranchée [illegible]	[illegible]
	[illegible]		Seven rounds were fired at the Faucky Road barrier.	[illegible]
	22.5.16		Four rounds were fired at the Barrier	[illegible]
	23.5.16		Six rounds were fired at the Faucky Road barrier [illegible] with the [illegible] of the barrier. [illegible] rounds [illegible] retaliation from the German large trench mortar	[illegible]
	24.5.16		Four rounds were fired at the Tranchée [illegible]	[illegible]
	[illegible]		[illegible]	

2449 Wt. W14957/M90 750,000 1/16 J.B.C. & A. Forms/C.2118/12.

Instructions regarding War Diaries and Intelligence Summaries are contained in F. S. Regs., Part II. and the Staff Manual respectively. Title Pages will be prepared in manuscript.

WAR DIARY
or
~~INTELLIGENCE SUMMARY~~
(Erase heading not required.)

Army Form C. 2118.

Place	Date	Hour	Summary of Events and Information	Remarks and references to Appendices
[illegible]	28.5.16		New position finished	[illegible]
	29.5.16		A reserve position commenced.	[illegible]
	30.5.16		New position Registered	[illegible]
	31.5.16		Man. firing was carried out from new position. The result seem good. Small pieces of timber were observed to fly from the enemies trench.	[illegible]

J.W. [illegible] Clarke Lieut
OC 43/1 TMB.

2449 Wt. W14957/M90 750,000 1/16 J.B.C. & A. Forms/C.2118/12.

Army Form C. 2118.

Instructions regarding War Diaries and Intelligence Summaries are contained in F. S. Regs., Part II. and the Staff Manual respectively. Title Pages will be prepared in manuscript.

WAR DIARY
or
~~INTELLIGENCE SUMMARY~~
(Erase heading not required.)

43/2 Trench Mortar Battery

Place	Date	Hour	Summary of Events and Information	Remarks and references to Appendices
In the Field	1916 May 1		During the day a new position was made & registered, ready for a night shoot, in conjunction with 3.7 & 2" Batteries. This Shoot took place about 10pm & was very successful. The enemy retaliated with 77mm Shells & heavy Shrapnel, but little material damage was done.	JH
	2 & 3rd		Retaliation to enemy Trench Mortars.	JH
	4th		30 rounds fired in retaliation	JH
		7.30pm	A Combined Shoot took place (Stokes 3.7 & 2" Medium) on the enemy front line, where new work had been in progress. The result was satisfactory	JH
	5th		New position built & registered on enemy's Sap (M.14 d. 7¾.4½ Sheet 51c SW1) 43 rounds fired in retaliation.	JH
	6th		22 rounds fired in retaliation	JH
	7th–8th		No firing took place owing to weather	
	9th	1pm	Fired 6 rounds at enemy working party & dispersed them	
	10th		Usual retaliation fire.	

2449 Wt. W14957/M90 750,000 1/16 J.B.C. & A. Forms/C.2118/12.

Army Form C. 2118.

WAR DIARY
or
~~INTELLIGENCE SUMMARY~~

(Erase heading not required.) 43/2 Trench Mortar Battery

Instructions regarding War Diaries and Intelligence Summaries are contained in F. S. Regs., Part II. and the Staff Manual respectively. Title Pages will be prepared in manuscript.

Place	Date	Hour	Summary of Events and Information	Remarks and references to Appendices
Field	11th	3pm.	1 Stokes Gun, 4.1-3.7, fired on enemy Sap (M14d 7¼ 4½). In the evening this was repeated, when enemy retaliated vigorously with heavy Shrapnel. It is supposed that a machine gun was put out of action, as no firing took place afterwards	JH
	12th to 21st		Usual retaliation fire.	
	22nd	5am.	Enemy fired for the first time, 1 large, + 1 medium MINENWERFER, apparently for the purpose of registering.	JH
			An enemy mine was discovered, under our front line. At request of General Cooper Cmdg 14th Div, 3 guns of this Battery were placed in defensive positions, in case the mine is exploded.	
	23rd to 31st		Retaliation fire.	
			Enemy's large mortars active	

Field
June 1st 1916

J. Hetherington Lieut
OC 43/2 Trench Mortar Bty

2449 Wt. W14957/M90 750,000 1/16 J.B.C. & A. Forms/C.2118/12.

Instructions regarding War Diaries and Intelligence Summaries are contained in F. S. Regs., Part II. and the Staff Manual respectively. Title Pages will be prepared in manuscript.

WAR DIARY
or
~~INTELLIGENCE SUMMARY~~
(Erase heading not required.)

Army Form C. 2118.

43/2 Trench Mortar Battery

Place	Date	Hour	Summary of Events and Information	Remarks and references to Appendices
In the Field.	1916 May 1		During the day a new position was made & registered ready for a night shoot, in conjunction with 3.7 & 2" Batteries. This Shoot took place about 10pm & was very successful. The enemy retaliated with 77mm. Shells, & heavy Shrapnel, but little material damage was done.	JH
	2 & 3rd		Retaliation to Enemy's Trench Mortar.	JH
	4th		30 rounds fired in retaliation	
		7/30pm	A Combined Shoot took place (Stokes, 3.7 & 2" Medium) on the enemy front line, where new work had been in progress. The result was Satisfactory (M.14 d. 7½.4½ Sheet 51B S.W.1)	JH.
	5th		New position built & registered on enemy's Sap. 43 rounds fired in retaliation.	JH
	6th		22 rounds fired in retaliation	JH
	7th-8th		No firing took place owing to weather	
	9th	10pm	Fired 6 rounds at enemy working party & dispersed them	
	10th		Usual retaliation fire.	

2449 Wt. W14957/M90 750,000 1/16 J.B.C. & A. Forms/C.2118/12.

43rd Trench Mortar Batt

42

43 T M Bty

Vol 4

Army Form C. 2118.

WAR DIARY
or
INTELLIGENCE SUMMARY

(Erase heading not required.)

Instructions regarding War Diaries and Intelligence Summaries are contained in F. S. Regs., Part II. and the Staff Manual respectively. Title Pages will be prepared in manuscript.

Place	Date	Hour	Summary of Events and Information	Remarks and references to Appendices
In the Field	1/6/16 – 16/6/16		Nothing of importance to report on these days	J.W.C.
"	17/6/16		Officers of the 164 Bde Trench Mortars arrived to see round trenches	J.W.C.
"	18/6/16		3130 rounds of Stoke ammunition arrived for this battery	J.W.C.
	19/6/16		Nothing to report	J.W.C.
"	20/6/16		Amalgamation of the two batteries 43/1 & 43/2	J.W.C.
	21/6/16 – 22/6/16		Nothing to report	J.W.C.
	23/6/16		43rd Trench Mortar Battery was relieved by the 164 Trench Mortar Battery. On the relief being complete the Battery proceeded to Billets in Arras	J.W.C.
	24/6/16		Two officers went up to the new trenches to see round them before taking over.	J.W.C.
	26/6/16 – 27/6/16		Battery was in reserve to the 95 Bde Trench Mortars	J.W.C.

2449 Wt. W14957/M90 750,000 1/16 J.B.C. & A. Forms/C.2118/12.

Instructions regarding War Diaries and Intelligence Summaries are contained in F. S. Regs., Part II. and the Staff Manual respectively. Title Pages will be prepared in manuscript.

WAR DIARY
or
~~INTELLIGENCE SUMMARY~~
2

(Erase heading not required.)

Army Form C. 2118.

Place	Date	Hour	Summary of Events and Information	Remarks and references to Appendices
In the Field	28/9/15		Half the Battery relieved the 95 Bde Trench Mortar Battery In the J. Sector N.W of ARRAS.	JPJ
"	29/9/15		Half the Battery proceeded to the 3rd Army Trench Mortar School to be rearmed with Stokes in place of the 3.7 guns which with they are armed	JPJ
"	30/9/15		Nothing to report.	
			J P Jenner Clark Lt OC 43rd Trench Mortar Batt	

2449 Wt. W14957/M90 750,000 1/16 J.B.C. & A. Forms/C.2118/12.

Army Form C. 2118.

Instructions regarding War Diaries and Intelligence Summaries are contained in F. S. Regs., Part II. and the Staff Manual respectively. Title Pages will be prepared in manuscript.

WAR DIARY
or
~~INTELLIGENCE SUMMARY~~

(Erase heading not required.) 43/2 Trench Mortar Battery.

Vol 4

Place	Date	Hour	Summary of Events and Information	Remarks and references to Appendices
Field	June 1st – 6th	–	Nothing special to report – Enemy very quiet slight retaliation fire.	
	7th	–	Enemy large T.M. active. – 14 rounds fired in retaliation.	
	8th – 21st	–	Usual retaliation fire.	
	22nd	–	This Battery came out of action from "G" sector, & moved to ARRAS. where they are remaining in support to the 95th Bde. T.M. Battery.	
	23rd	–	This Battery together with 43/1 Bty were absorbed, & in future will be known as 43rd Bde Trench Mortar Battery.	

Field
24/6/16

J Hetherington Lieut
OC 43/2 Trench Mortar Battery

2449 Wt. W14957/M90 750,000 1/16 J.B.C. & A. Forms/C.2118/12.

Instructions regarding War Diaries and Intelligence Summaries are contained in F. S. Regs., Part II. and the Staff Manual respectively. Title Pages will be prepared in manuscript.

WAR DIARY
or
~~INTELLIGENCE SUMMARY~~

Army Form C. 2118.

(Erase heading not required.) 43/2 Trench Mortar Battery.

Place	Date	Hour	Summary of Events and Information	Remarks and references to Appendices
Field	June 1st–6th	–	Nothing special to report – Enemy very quiet. Slight retaliation fire.	
	7th	–	Enemy large T.M. active. – 14 rounds fired in retaliation.	
	8th – 21st	–	Usual retaliation fire.	
	22nd	–	This Battery came out of action from "G" sector, & moved to ARRAS where they are remaining in support to the 95th Bde. T.M. Battery.	
	23rd	–	This Battery together with 43/1 Bty were absorbed, & in future will be known as 43rd Bde Trench Mortar Battery.	

Field
24/6/16

J Hetherington Lieut
O.C. 43/2 Trench Mortar Battery

2449 Wt. W14957/M90 750,000 1/16 J.B.C. & A. Forms/C.2118/12.

Army Form C. 2118.

Instructions regarding War Diaries and Intelligence Summaries are contained in F. S. Regs., Part II. and the Staff Manual respectively. Title Pages will be prepared in manuscript.

WAR DIARY
or
~~INTELLIGENCE SUMMARY~~
(Erase heading not required.)

43/2 Trench Mortar Battery

Place	Date	Hour	Summary of Events and Information	Remarks and references to Appendices
Field	11th	3pm.	1 Stokes Gun, 4.1-3.7", fired on enemy Sap ~~Hd~~ (M14d. 7¼ · 4½). In the evening this was repeated, when enemy retaliated vigorously with heavy Shrapnel. It is supposed that a machine gun was put out of action, as no firing took place afterwards	JH
	12th to 21st		Usual retaliation fire.	
	22nd	5am,	Enemy fired for the first time, 1 large, + 1 medium MINENWERFER, apparently for the purpose of registering.	JH
			An enemy mine was discovered, under our front line. At request of General Cooper Cmdg 14th Div, 3 guns of this Battery were placed in defensive positions, in case the mine is exploded.	
	23rd to 31st		Retaliation fire. Enemys large mortars active	

Field
June 1st 1916

J. Hetherington Lieut
OC 43/2 Trench Mortar Bty

2449 Wt. W14957/M90 750,000 1/16 J.B.C. & A. Forms/C.2118/12.

43rd Trench Mortar Batt.

WAR DIARY
or
INTELLIGENCE SUMMARY
(Erase heading not required.)

Army Form C. 2118.

Instructions regarding War Diaries and Intelligence Summaries are contained in F. S. Regs., Part II. and the Staff Manual respectively. Title Pages will be prepared in manuscript.

Place	Date	Hour	Summary of Events and Information	Remarks and references to Appendices
[illegible]	1/6/16 – 16/6/16		Nothing of importance to report on these days.	[illegible]
"	17/6/16		Officers of the 16th Bde Trench Mortar arrived to see round trenches	[illegible]
"	18/6/16		3130 rounds of Stokes ammunition arrived for the battery	[illegible]
	19/6/16		Nothing to report	[illegible]
	20/6/16		Amalgamation of the two batteries 43/1 & 43/2	[illegible]
	21/6/16 – 22/6/16		Nothing to report	[illegible]
	23/6/16		43rd Trench Mortar Battery was relieved by the 16th Trench Mortar Battery. On the relief being complete the Battery proceeded to Billets in Arras	[illegible]
	24/6/16		Two officers went up to the new trenches to see round them before taking over.	[illegible]
	25/6/16 – 27/6/16		Battery was in reserve to the 45 Bde Trench Mortar	

2449 Wt. W14957/M90 750,000 1/16 J.B.C. & A. Forms/C.2118/12.

43rd Trench Mortar Batt.

Instructions regarding War Diaries and Intelligence Summaries are contained in F. S. Regs., Part II. and the Staff Manual respectively. Title Pages will be prepared in manuscript.

WAR DIARY
or
~~INTELLIGENCE SUMMARY~~
(Erase heading not required.)

Army Form C. 2118.

Place	Date	Hour	Summary of Events and Information	Remarks and references to Appendices
In the Field	1/6/16 – 16/6/16		Nothing of importance to report on these days!!!	J.W.C.
"	17/6/16		Officers of the 164 Bde Trench Mortars arrived to see round trenches	J.W.C.
"	18/6/16		3130 rounds of Stoke ammunition arrived for this battery	J.W.C.
	19/6/16		Nothing to report	J.W.C.
	20/6/16		Amalgamation of the two batteries 43/1 & 43/2	J.W.C.
	21/6/16 – 21/6/16		Nothing to report	J.W.C.
	23/6/16		43rd Trench Mortar Battery was relieved by the 164 Trench Mortar Battery. On the relief being complete the Battery proceeded to Billets in Arras.	J.W.C.
	24/6/16		Two officers went up to the new trenches to see round them before taking over.	J.W.C.
	25/6/16 – 27/6/16		Battery was in reserve to the 95 Bde Trench Mortars	

2449 Wt. W14957/M90 750,000 1/16 J.B.C. & A. Forms/C.2118/12.

Instructions regarding War Diaries and Intelligence Summaries are contained in F. S. Regs., Part II. and the Staff Manual respectively. Title Pages will be prepared in manuscript.

WAR DIARY 2

or

~~INTELLIGENCE SUMMARY~~

(Erase heading not required.)

Army Form C. 2118.

Place	Date	Hour	Summary of Events and Information	Remarks and references to Appendices
In Line	25/9/15		Half the Battery returned the 95 Bde Trench Mortar Battery In the J sector N.W of ARRAS.	[illegible]
"	28/9/15		Half the Battery proceeded to the 3rd Army Trench Mortar School to be rearmed with Stokes in place of the 3.7 guns which with they were armed	[illegible]
	30/9/15		nothing to report	

J. Jenner Clarke Lt

OC 43rd Trench Mortar Batt

2449 Wt. W14957/M90 750,000 1/16 J.B.C. & A. Forms/C.2118/12.

Instructions regarding War Diaries and Intelligence Summaries are contained in F. S. Regs., Part II. and the Staff Manual respectively. Title Pages will be prepared in manuscript.

WAR DIARY 2
or
~~INTELLIGENCE SUMMARY~~
(Erase heading not required.)

Army Form C. 2118.

Place	Date	Hour	Summary of Events and Information	Remarks and references to Appendices
In the Field	25/6/15		Half the Battery relieved the 95 Bde Trench Mortar Battery In the 'J' sector N.W of ARRAS.	JBJ
"	29/6/15		Half the Battery proceeded to the 3rd Army Trench Mortar School to be rearmed with Stokes in place of the 3.7 guns which with they were armed	JB
	30/6/15		Nothing to report.	

J B Jenner Clark Lt
OC 43rd Trench Mortar Bat.

2449 Wt. W14957/M90 750,000 1/16 J.B.C. & A. Forms/C.2118/12.

Instructions regarding War Diaries and Intelligence Summaries are contained in F. S. Regs., Part II. and the Staff Manual respectively. Title Pages will be prepared in manuscript.

WAR DIARY
or
~~INTELLIGENCE SUMMARY~~

(Erase heading not required.) 43/2 Trench Mortar Battery.

Dupl

Army Form C. 2118.

Place	Date	Hour	Summary of Events and Information	Remarks and references to Appendices
Field	June 1st to 6th	–	Nothing special to report – Enemy very quiet. Slight retaliation fire.	
	7th	–	Enemy large T.M. active. – 14 rounds fired in retaliation.	
	8th to 21st	–	Usual retaliation fire.	
	22nd	–	This Battery came out of action from G. sector & moved to ARRAS where they are remaining in support to the 95th Bde. T.M. Battery.	
	23rd	–	This Battery together with 43/1 Bty were absorbed & in future will be known as 43rd Bde Trench Mortar Battery.	

Field
24/6/16

J. Hetherington Lieut
OC 43/2 Trench Mortar Battery

2449 Wt. W14957/M90 750,000 1/16 J.B.C. & A. Forms/C.2118/12.

43 Trench Mortar Batt.

WAR DIARY
or
~~INTELLIGENCE SUMMARY~~

(Erase heading not required.)

1

Army Form C. 2118.

Instructions regarding War Diaries and Intelligence Summaries are contained in F. S. Regs., Part II. and the Staff Manual respectively. Title Pages will be prepared in manuscript.

Place	Date	Hour	Summary of Events and Information	Remarks and references to Appendices
Field	1.7.16		Half of the 43rd Trench Mortar Battery relieved the 95th TM Batt in the J sector	
	4.7.16		Half the 43 TMB returned from the TM School bringing with them 4 3" Stokes mortars	
	5.7.16		Half the Battery took over J 1 subsector & proceeded to dig positions	
	7.7.16		The 3.7 mortars with which the battery had been armed were returned to the D.A.D.O.S	
	8.7.16		Three rounds were fired on this day.	
	9.7.16		Ten rounds were fired	
	10.7.16		Two guns of this Battery stood by to support a Trench Raid carried out by the 6th Kings Own Yorkshire L.I. The raid was postponed	
	19.7.16		A shoot was carried out by the 6" Hows on a point in the German trenches. The battery stood by to retaliate to enemy's trench mortars Twenty six rounds were fired	
	21.7.16		Five rounds were fired in retaliation to enemy's Trench Mortar	
			Two men of this Battery were wounded by a rifle grenade	
	22.7.16		Thirty rounds were fired on this day.	

[illegible] Trench Mortar Battery

Instructions regarding War Diaries and Intelligence Summaries are contained in F. S. Regs., Part II. and the Staff Manual respectively. Title Pages will be prepared in manuscript.

WAR DIARY
or
INTELLIGENCE SUMMARY

(Erase heading not required.)

Army Form C. 2118.

2

Place	Date	Hour	Summary of Events and Information	Remarks and references to Appendices
In the Field	23.7.16		A raid was made by the enemy on our trenches. [illegible] Forty six rounds were fired. One gun was struck in the bombardment & damaged so badly that it had to be sent down to the DADOS. A large quantity of ammunition was also buried.	[illegible]
	24.7.16		One hundred & eighty four rounds were fired on the day.	[illegible]
	25.7.16		Sixty seven rounds were fired.	[illegible]
	[illegible]		[illegible] Battery was relieved by representatives of the [illegible] & proceeded by motor lorries from ARRAS to WARLUZ where we remained till the 30th.	[illegible]
	30.7.16		The Battery marched with the Brigade to REMAISNIL	[illegible]

J W Turner [illegible] Clarke Capt.
OC 48th Trench Mortar Batt.

2449 Wt. W14957/M90 750,000 1/16 J.B.C. & A. Forms/C.2118/12.

43 Trench Mortar Batt. 1

Army Form C. 2118.

WAR DIARY
or
~~INTELLIGENCE SUMMARY~~

(Erase heading not required.)

Instructions regarding War Diaries and Intelligence Summaries are contained in F. S. Regs., Part II. and the Staff Manual respectively. Title Pages will be prepared in manuscript.

Place	Date	Hour	Summary of Events and Information	Remarks and references to Appendices
Field	1.7.16		Half of the 43rd Trench Mortar Battery relieved the 95th T.M. Batt'n the 'J' Sector	JWC
	4.7.16		Half the 43 TMB returned from the T.M. School bringing with them 4. 3" 'Stokes' Mortars	JWC
	5.7.16		Half the Battery took over 'J'1 Subsector & proceeded to dig positions	JWC
	7.7.16		The 3.7 mortars with which the battery had been armed were returned to the DADOS	JWC JWC
	8.7.16		Three rounds were fired on this day.	JWC
	9.7.16		Ten rounds were fired	
	13.7.16		Two guns of this battery stood by to support a Trench Raid carried out by the 6th Kings Own Yorkshire L.I. The raid was postponed	JWC
	19.7.16		A shoot was carried out by the 6" Hows on a point in the German trenches. The battery stood by to retaliate to enemy's trench mortars. Twenty six rounds were fired	JWC
	21.7.16		Five rounds were fired in retaliation to enemy's Trench Mortar. Two men of this battery were wounded by a rifle grenade	JWC
	22.7.16		Thirty rounds were fired on this day	JWC

43 Trench Mortar Batt. 1

Instructions regarding War Diaries and Intelligence Summaries are contained in F. S. Regs., Part II. and the Staff Manual respectively. Title Pages will be prepared in manuscript.

WAR DIARY
or
~~INTELLIGENCE SUMMARY~~
(Erase heading not required.)

Army Form C. 2118.

Place	Date	Hour	Summary of Events and Information	Remarks and references to Appendices
Field	1.7.16		Half of the 43rd Trench Mortar Battery relieved the 95 th T M Batt in the 'J' Sector	J.W.C.
	4.7.16		Half the 43 TMB returned from the T M School bringing with them 4. 3" Stokes' Mortars	J.W.C.
	5.7.16		Half the Battery took over 'J'1 Subsector & proceeded to dig positions	J.W.C.
	7.7.16		The 3.7 mortars with which the battery had been armed were returned to the DADOS	J.W.C.
	8.7.16		Three rounds were fired on this day.	J.W.C.
	9.7.16		Ten rounds were fired	J.W.C.
	13.7.16		Two guns of this battery stood by to support a Trench Raid carried out by the 6th Kings Own Yorkshire L I The raid was postponed	J.W.C.
	19.7.16		A shoot was carried out by the 6" Hows on a point in the German trenches. The battery stood by to retaliate to enemy's trench mortars. Twenty six rounds were fired	J.W.C.
	21.7.16		Five rounds were fired in retaliation to enemy Trench Mortar Two men of this battery were wounded by a rifle grenade	J.W.C.
	22.7.16		Thirty rounds were fired on the day	J.W.C.

2449 Wt. W14957/M90 750,000 1/16 J.B.C. & A. Forms/C.2118/12.

4.3rd Trench Mortar Battery

WAR DIARY
or
~~INTELLIGENCE~~ SUMMARY

(*Erase heading not required.*)

2

Army Form C. 2118.

Instructions regarding War Diaries and Intelligence Summaries are contained in F. S. Regs., Part II. and the Staff Manual respectively. Title Pages will be prepared in manuscript.

Place	Date	Hour	Summary of Events and Information	Remarks and references to Appendices
In the Field	23.7.16		A raid was made by the enemy on our trenches ~~Twenty~~ Forty six rounds were fired. One gun was buried in the bombardment & damaged so badly that it had to be sent down to the DADOS. A large quantity of ammunition was also buried	JWJC
	24.7.16		One hundred & eighty four rounds were fired on the day	JWJC
	25.7.16		Sixty Seven rounds were fired	JWJC
	28.7.16		The battery was relieved by representatives of the 110th Bde & 62nd T.M. Bde & proceeded by motor lorries from ARRAS to WARLUZEL where we remained ~~for a day~~ till the 30th	JWJC
	30.7.16		The Battery marched with the Brigade to REMAISNIL	JWJC

J W Jenner Clarke Capt
OC 43rd Trench Mortar Batt

2449 Wt. W14957/M90 750,000 1/16 J.B.C. & A. Forms/C.2118/12.

4.3rd Trench Mortar Battery

Instructions regarding War Diaries and Intelligence Summaries are contained in F. S. Regs., Part II. and the Staff Manual respectively. Title Pages will be prepared in manuscript.

WAR DIARY
or
~~INTELLIGENCE SUMMARY~~

(Erase heading not required.)

2

Army Form C. 2118.

Place	Date	Hour	Summary of Events and Information	Remarks and references to Appendices
In the Field	23.7.16		A raid was made by the enemy on our trenches. ~~Twenty~~ Forty six rounds were fired. One gun was buried in the bombardment & damaged so badly that it had to be sent down to the DADOS. A large quantity of ammunition was also buried	JWJC
	24.7.16		One hundred & eighty four rounds were fired on this day	JWJC
	25.7.16		Sixty Seven rounds were fired	JWJC
	28.7.16		The battery was relieved by representatives of the 110th Bde & 62nd I.Bde. & proceeded by motor lorries from ARRAS to WARLUZEL where we remained ~~for one day~~ till the 30th.	JWJC
	30.7.16		The Battery marched with the Brigade to TEMAISNIL	JWJC

JWJenner. Clarke Capt
OC 43rd Trench Mortar Batt

2449 Wt. W14957/M90 750,000 1/16 J.B.C. & A. Forms/C.2118/12.

www.ingramcontent.com/pod-product-compliance
Lightning Source LLC
Chambersburg PA
CBHW081447160426
43193CB00013B/2405